ZOOLOGICAL
Ali's Palace
Site of Fustat

NEW MAP
OF
CAIRO
AND ENVIRONS
SCALE = 1:15.000
by
Eng. A. NICOHOSOFF
18 Bld. ZAGHLOUL,
ALEXANDRIA
P.T. 15

LUNA PARK HOTEL CAIRO
SEMIRAMIS
CAIRO HÔTEL
HOTEL CECIL
ALEXANDRIA
EGYPT
Proprietors
METZGER
CRUISE OF THE "LOTUS"
The Supreme Egyptian Tour
1931
EGYPT
RED SEA
BUREAU OF UNIVERSITY TRAVEL
11 Boyd Street, Newton, Massachusetts
Paris Office: 3 Rue du Mont-Thabor
CAIRO
EGYPT
SHEPHEARD'S
HOTEL
RIVER NILE
Imbaba Br.
Police Sta.
Bulaq
Ez. el Zamalik
Hockey Ground
Ez. Aguza
Y.M.C.A. Sports Club
Coptic Trades Sch.
English Sch.
St. Paul's Ch.
Garden City

S E A
Beirut
P. Said
Alexandria
Cairo
Suez
El Kargeh
1st Cat

PLAYER'S
Q.CLEOPATRA
P.NEFERT.
K.RAMESES III
Q.AMENARTAS
QUEEN AMENOPHIS
K.AMENOPHIS.
Q.HATSHEPSET
QUEEN MAKERI.
QUEEN AAHMES
Q.ARSINOE.II
K.THOTHMES.III
K.SETI.I
CIGARETTES

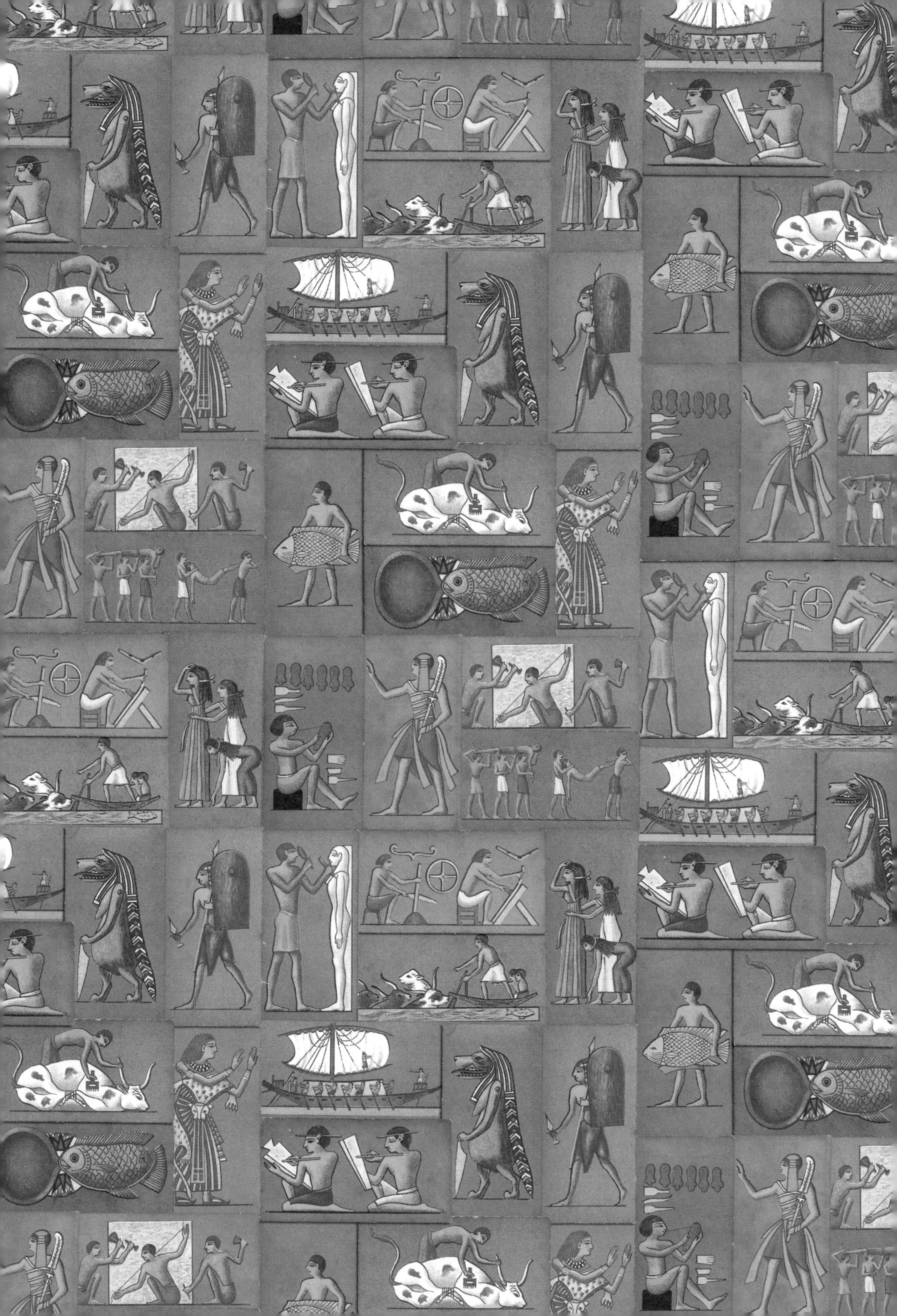

EGYPT
N
S
E
W
ALEXANDRIA
CAIRO
DENDERA
PYRAMIDS AND SPHINX
SAKKARA
Shadouf
ARABIAN DESERT
LIBYAN DESERT
Caravan
THEBES
ASSIUT
BENI HASSAN
ABYDOS
KARNAK
Oasis
LUXOR
MEDINET HABU
KOM OMBO
EDFU
ASSUAN
Quarry
PHILAE
Plowing
SHELLAL
KASR IBRIM
Ibis
ABU SIMBEL
ES SEBUA
Felucca

EGYPT
N
S
E
W
ABYDOS
KARNAK
LUXOR
MEDINET HABU
EDFU
KOM OMBO
ASSUAN
PHILAE
SHELLAL
KASR IBRIM
ABU SIMBEL
ES SEBUA
ALEXANDRIA
CAIRO
DENDERA
PYRAMIDS AND SPHINX
SAKKARA
ARABIAN DESERT
LIBYAN DESERT
THEBES
ASSIUT
BENI HASSAN
Oasis
Quarry
Plowing
Ibis
Felucca
Shadouf
Caravan